Always Look
for the

Tessy Gold Starry

GOLD STARRY EDITIONS

ISBN: Softcover   978-1-5245-9466-4
        EBook   978-1-5245-9465-7

Print information available on the last page

Rev. date: 11/16/2016

To order additional copies of this book, contact:
Xlibris
0800-056-3182
www.xlibrispublishing.co.uk
Orders@ Xlibrispublishing.co.uk

ADDITIONAL AUTHOR'S NOTES

My poetry book looks at the importance of childhood, genetic roots and the shaping of identity. Additionally, the simplicity of the natural world and animals is portrayed in a humorous way. Poetically they are playful, musical and engaging for children and adults but particularly children under any form of controlling restraint or who want to explore their identity further.

The poems also explore energy exchange, musicality frequencies and consciousness. Predominant themes featured are positivity and freedom against any form of adversity: particularly psychological control, a seemingly invisible yet very present danger and obstacle to people realizing their true potential.

Tessy Gold Starry

Table of Contents

Stale dusk.

Like sticky tar, an empty tray
Burned out ash,
Empty words sit in the trash,
A smear of dirt, on broken glass
Or a plate that has been passed to me with served up memories -
Gone- relief at last.

While stale rose petals fall,
On yesterday's shawl,
Covering ivory skin glisten,
In the night 's hum listen
As cricket slumbers and skips,
Through blades of grass peering
At rosy lips,
Serene and clean

But with yesterday's sheen
And early morning dew
Spares only a few
So pick energy with care
As fluorescent flairs light up
Electric invisible lairs

Behind what we feel –

Love, break or steal.

Ratitatcat.

Ratitatcat the rat ran away with the cat.
The clock struck one.
The vet has a son.

Ratittty Catitty Splat!

Ratitatcat the rat ran away with the cat.
The clock struck five.
Feeling alive.

Ratittty Catitty Splat!

Ratitatcat the rat away with the cat,
The clock struck ten,
And ran up Big Ben.

Ratittty Catitty Splat!

Where is the rat that proposed to the cat
That chased the vet that I just met?

Where is my tea near the apple tree
In Linden Lea that would help me to see
And have empathy...

With the rat,

the cat

and the vet!

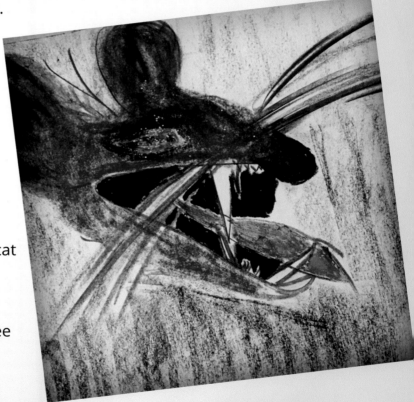

Fresh Dew.

Fresh dew wakes my soul
Your words sit on my heart, still.
Once forlorn, now peace.

Seven Haiku's in fifteen minutes.

Glassy reflection –
Sun shaft of the soul surging
Through grass-berry clouds.

Pillow, canopy
Willow tree embroidery,
Hypnotic touch, soft paint brush

Paints the scene, teal green
Beauty unseen, swans for ever
Blissful together –

Sun shadow, rust glow
Amber snippets reside
Giggling crickets

Hide my love, silent
Like fading twilight
A baby's nightlight.

Sleeping slumber
Pluck blackberry crumberly,
Words, dew on my heart.

Bull rush, tawny plush
Breathe secrets of silk side
Moon lit sea, hush – tide.

Mary Rose Ship.

It was her anchor that sank her,
On the sea of deceipt
No receipt –
Just disappearance of her,
Bow and Stern under clear sea bathe,
Even the white horses trotting the tips
of the waves

Could not save -
Tonnes of water
Ought to have sought her
But descended over dry rot of the years
Water into tears,
A clustice of justice
Seeing Law from the shore
A sharp claw running through the
debate
Of her fate

Sails set a'glow –
My fiend and my foe
A pirate flag of fear
Hoisted up the rear

The coots tried to save
Her watery grave
But the boat sank

With truth in her tank

Rotting algae and rank
Stirring seaweed so damp
Seashells a' dozen
Waves goodbye to her cousin

Free legal aid
Watery fade
Ocean grave

Truth glisten and fade
A game that was played
Chess pawns that were laid

On ship beams
Sun gleams
Master the faster cracking plaster
Waving farewell to disaster

Resurrected in 1982 or 81
The battle was won-
Salvaged she was,
Away from enemy and foes,

Our beautiful Mary Rose.

Noughts and Crosses.

Noughts and crosses,
Criss Cross,
Win or Loss,

Like life,
A game to lose or win,
To dance and spin.
Or curse in the bin.

Like a vegetable peel
Or a thief that will try to steal
Your soul...

Or lure you into a mind trap
Cheese to a rat
Juicy and FAT!

Noughts and crosses
Criss Cross
Win or loss.

Play again
On the edge of life

To win. To strive
On the edge of the knife!

But don't look back
Give your old life the sack
Look forward
Into your heart
Make a start

And gallop away on the tips of your
dreams
Rushing like streams
Star glitter moonbeams
Lighting the way
Like the yellow brick road
Without a heavy load.

A star.
Whirling, twirling, curling
Across the sky.

Where infinite dreams lie.

Spider catchers.

Castles, forests, peace, sleep.
Dewy spider webs
Glistening in the sun rays.
Don't tear down such an intricate work of art.
It's too pretty and the only way the spider
Can make food to survive.
Soft webs that can catch and ensnare
Flies to devour.
Sticky yet silky
Soft and spinderly
Rapunzel let down your long hair
Your prince will
Climb up and save you
Like the faithful Collie
Saved Jemima Puddle-duck.
Spiders are your friends

BUT

Watch out for the spider catchers
Like knights in shining armour
Running to your rescue
Whilst THEIR web glistens in the sun's

Early morning dew.

Autumn.

Autumn leaves sweep away thoughts,
Once sat heavy and motionless,
In narrow gutters.

Autumn leaves sweep away-
Yesterday's regrets,
Once amidst with dust
And rotting fruit
Now swept clean -

By Autumn's team circling –
Wind, crashing thunder,
The stage set of life,
Camera's a'blaze-
With golden, red light.

A crunching carpet of leaves
The homes of insects,
Birds and coots,

Lining their nests,
Happy, not aggrieved.

Autumn winds sweep away
Drain pipe blocks -
In the mind
That previously made me blind-
Tumbling keys now undoing the locks
Releasing the shocks..

Electricity is in the air,
You just can't see -
The delicates layer

Whirling, twirling, curling
Silver pearlising of rain –

Yesterday's nasty's
Washed away down the drain.

Withering leaves.

Withering leaves-
Like the soft edges of my heart,
Falling away to a new start,
Blossoming trees; cherries, passion fruit and bees.

Withering leaves-
Like the bright ray of morning sun,
Sleepy eyes, the soft spring breeze,
Children, curious on their knees

Withering leaves-
Like emergence of moonlight,
Moon rays-
Shining on solid bricks and tiles,
Mud and piles of more

Withering leaves,
Scattering seeds,
Babies feeds,

Withering leaves hiding in the eaves of yesterday's
Whisper and clasp

Letting go of the past.

Locks and Keys.

Fumbling keys in nasty locks,
I had to appease,
Dusty cobweb- peering spider eye
"Open the door please-
Let's all comply."

Fumbling keys in broken locks
Open the doors
No dreams can you seize -
"The steps are icy," remarks Fox
Devouring the flocks.

Fumbling keys in iron gates,
Swinging open in haste,
Little dangers to face,
Cold, stone floors
A still-ness in silence.

Glistening red heather
On remote rugged moors,
A glad separation,
To write and retreat

Plump up the sofa
Resting my feet
Figurines in the fire,
Lighting desire,
Crackling flame
Burning away pain –

Fumbling keys in golden locks,
Disgarding the shocks,
Binning the box,

Infiltrating the room with
Damp, green gloom -

A foggy mist
An unfulfilled list

But not anymore!

I opened the door...

When I am a multimillionaire.

When I am a multimillionaire
I will buy those dear to my heart
A loving fresh start –
Houses they can maintain,
A sanctuary from pain.

When I am a multimillionaire
I will give to many charities
With warmth compassion
Smiles and hilarity.

When I am a multimillionaire
I will buy a house in Whitby
Sail and row on the sea
And enjoy the sunset
Whilst eating my tea.

When I am a multimillionaire
I will do an attic conversion
And relax with Maine coons
And with Persians
By a crackling fire, write and inspire.

When I am a multimillionaire
Money I can invest

But love is the richness
That is always the best.

When I am a multimillionaire
I will wear scruffy leggings
And not turn my nose up and try to
compete.
I would write every day
And avoid the Elite.

When I am a multimillionaire
I will create libraries and even more
schools
And positive artwork,
Not negative fools
Swimming in the poison of everyday
news,
Waiting in crowds or waiting in
queues...

To be told what's next
Or even the best.
This is my dream,
And with mistakes, I'll succeed.

Always look for the Blue Sky.

Always look for the blue sky,
When the clouds descend.
The grey army hides the
Blue sky lens.

Always look for the blue sky,
When army mists meet up for battle,
And the farmer rapidly summons in his
cattle-

Always look for the blue sky.
Glitter rays of golden sun,
Love the people
As they reject and shun.

Always look for the blue skies.
Love the people,
When they criticize and shut their eyes,
Repressing cries under deceit and lies,

Always look for the blue sky.
One day our spirit will rise so high,
Into the blue we will ascend,
No money here can we spend,

So take the chance while you can,
To make a stand,
Love with your heart,
It can start.

Always look for the blue skies,
Releasing damaging soul ties,
Allow your spirit to fly away,
No longer shy, it can sing and play,

The days of your life,
Free as a kite,
Soaring in flight.

Guilty Swamp Monster.

Guilty swamp monster
Knows his mind,
Swamping people, not being kind.
Let's hope he is sorry for his deliberate
crimes,
And undoes all those swampy slimes,
Or lost he will be
Into fires of hell shall
He descend,

And no truths there will he be able to
bend,
Because in heaven and hell there's no
keeping score,

Everyone is humble,

Rich, no more.

A Cat's Life.

All of a snuggle,
Bathing in rainbow pools of light,
And afternoon hush,
Catching the light droplets,
Leaping off crystal edges,
A playful scamper,
A quiet nip of the tail-
Bundling down the stairs
In pairs
Tails swishing in time
While breakfast is served
Fresh meat and treats
And dry food.
Litter is cleaned.
So between food and sunbathe
And play
Cat dreams of mice and gardens
And underground tunnels
And a tile roof.
Their thoughts dancing
Well into the afternoon
With playful glee
And mystery
Asleep once more
Dreaming of early morning
Light delights through
The moon shone night
Cat whiskers sensing, prickling

The spirits of the night
And guarding till morn
The early dew
Sits quietly on the
Misty dawn
Crickets hiding
On fresh crab apple lawn.
As cat will sit and yawn.

Sydney the banana-eating snail.

Sydney the banana-eating snail
Had a very sweet tail.
He resisted the carrot
And sat on the parrot
Eating his piece of banana

Sydney the banana-eating snail
Had a very sticky trail.
He ate up the sunflowers
And stole the fairies' powers
Eating his piece of banana.

Sydney the banana-eating snail
Liked to write and receive mail.
He wrote a letter to the universe

And got thoroughly immersed
Eating his piece of banana.

Sydney the banana-eating snail
Was so cool
He sat on a stool
And attended the writing group
Eating his piece of banana.

Sydney the banana-eating snail
Went back to the wild,
His shell back intact.
He's happy now making magical snail trails
Eating his piece of banana.

The Gypsy's child.

An education from Cambridge
University,
Like a silky shawl, hides from view
All beneath.

Like layers of an onion,
Roots deep in fertile soil,
Peeling back the years,
And the culture.

Hidden, from view,
Masked with an accent
Voice un-mistakenly English.

As crystal glitters in sun wash,
And horses glance,
The hushed words of today.

Of the smell of the fields
And morning dew
Wheels and beautiful faces,

Painting the Cant language of a whole
generation-
Gone.

Erosion of culture -
Where much could be learnt

Of sharing, listening, music and telling
stories.
Independent thinking and skills,
Strength and fortitude
The highest creativity -

At one with the land, sea and the sky.

Silently fighting -

Today's prejudice.

Mixed Race.

A mixed race,
You can't tell from her face.
The mother tongue,
Has not yet won in word
But is definitely heard in other ways,
Marked by the days-

The clip clip of horses hooves,
On hot, tin, metal roofs,
Delicate paint stroke-

From Gyspy folk,
A copper kettle,
On a burning stove,
Dolls house furniture
Sits in an alcove.

A mixed race.
You can't tell from her face,
Or a voice so English,
Public Schools,
A mask of jewels-

Hides a society
That doesn't play by most people's
rules
Rather, builds their own lives with their
own tools

Fertile farm lands,
Swapping food for farm hands.

The accepting earth-
Shows gratitude-
Rich food,
For many mouths,
The curious cows
Observe the Vardo's curves-

While twilight creeps,
And sun breath seeps,
Through waking trees
Black-bird glance appease
Rustled gold-brown leaves
Crunch Scrunch!
A snail's lunch - he is fed.
While sun glow-
Blankets the sky,
With starry bed.

And crystal glint
Lighting brick and flint

The Gypsy watches all
With her sparking shawl.

Maggie May.

Maggie May,
As clear as day,
Made of clay,
A horse's bray.

Maggie May,
Born in 1937,
Rain from heaven.

Maggie May,
Married Jack McAleer,
As the days drew nearer,
Pictures are clearer,

Paintbrush their lives-
In herbs like chives,
Bitter sweet flowers,
Fairies powers,

Leaping through saffron
Grasses and meadows wild,
Dandelion sun glow,
Child after child.

The stove is burning-
Coal alight
Dusky animals creeping
As days turn to night.

The hum of crickets,
And the breath of willow,
Apple and cherry trees,
Breeze on my pillow,

Horses whiskers shiver-
A feast of hay,
Friendly farmers deliver,
The awakening day

Fire flies; dull eyes,
Hopelessly poor,
Tom cats claw,
Scratching on the door.

Swung open-
To bright stitch,
Dazzling the dull ditch nearby,
An artists eye.

Don't deny or even try-
To defeat this soul,
You'll end up in a big black hole.

As she sits nicely in the skies-
Shining brightly,
Huge dragon flies descend,
Beautiful wings can't bend.

Maggie May protects her child
Through cloud tiled wishes,
And darting fishes,
Sun rays glisten-

You just have to listen.

McAleer, Dixon, Jackson,

Names are funny things,
We don't choose them,
They are chosen for us-
From birth out of the earth
And each name is not the same
And sends a different picture into minds of different kinds.

Names are funny things
I suppose when we are older we could change them,
Or if we become artists, writers, peace makers or fighters

Names are funny things,
Yet they mean a lot
Like McAleer rhymes with Shakespeare
And Dixon with fix'em
And Jackson with Daxson
And Walshy with Bulchy

All giving a unique vibration
Or a musical beat

Notes on a sheet!

The Curious Cow.

The curious cow
Peers at the morning dew,
Blades of grass
Waving farewell.
Spider's whisper
Ushering the flies'
Twinkling web of disguise
Sun rays dance
In river time.

Bulrushes smile
Soft velvet touch;
Feathers glide
Through half spoken air;
Electric cords
Invisible, layer on layer
Caressing crab apple
Blossoming pirouette.

Under the ripe sun's glaze
Rainbow crystals
Searching for dreams
Emergence of moonlight

The curious cow sees all.

Rose my heart.

Rose my heart,
My love, my sweet stone,
Are you hiding in the trees,
Are you smiling?
Smiling just for me,
A beauty. The rock –
Rock of my life.
Rock of strife.

Box frame.
No train!
Yes fame!
And it came
Without shame,
Without pain.

Scribble-Liddle the cat and the Diddle,
Ran off with the fiddle,
Forgetting his middle,
Skiddadle – he got it back,
Quick as a cat,
With a flowing mane
And no pain.

The Father in my head.

The father in my head,
Occasionally boils lead,

He welcomes me round,
Without a sound -

Loves, hugs, encouraging me,
Wisdom, kindness and love to see,

The father in my head
"Congratulations!" He said.

When my first book was there,
Happiness kindness, pride an
unspoken air.

The father in my head said, "Yes
you are blessed."

The father in my head
Encouraged me to see
What's right for me,

And writing it will be!

The father in my head
Is always open, warm-hearted and kind,
To anger, he is truly blind...

The father in my head replied
"You can do anything you want to," he
cried.

Be a success so just believe,
And out of the darkness you will leave,
All the days of your life,
No need for strife,

Just show your talent,
It's just a matter of time...
No need to pine.

Let your life unwind,

In its wonderful design.

Fairy blessing.

As fairy dances in the sunlight's ray,
Children sit and play,
Every fairy blest the cherry tree,
And let me see,
The red roses climb the bricks so strong,
Their petals all summer have I longed.
Crab apple send their blessings; honey makes then sweet;
And bumble bees buzz and pollinate,
Near the garden seat.
As the day breaks and the sunny dawn,
Meets the fairies' tea party on crab apple lawn,
Peace now, not disturbed
Robin taking a little bath in the puddle
What a sweet little bird

Ever shall I love this place,
Its garden southwest face.

Wild flower meadow to my right,
More crab apple trees in my sight.

Thank you for this wonderful abode,
A sanctuary free from heavy load

Crystals reflect the light
While spirit takes rest from the fight.

I wonder!

There was a smoke bear
In my lair
And a shadow
With lots of hair,
Not to mention
A bubble bear.
I wonder what's hiding
Behind my kitchen chair!

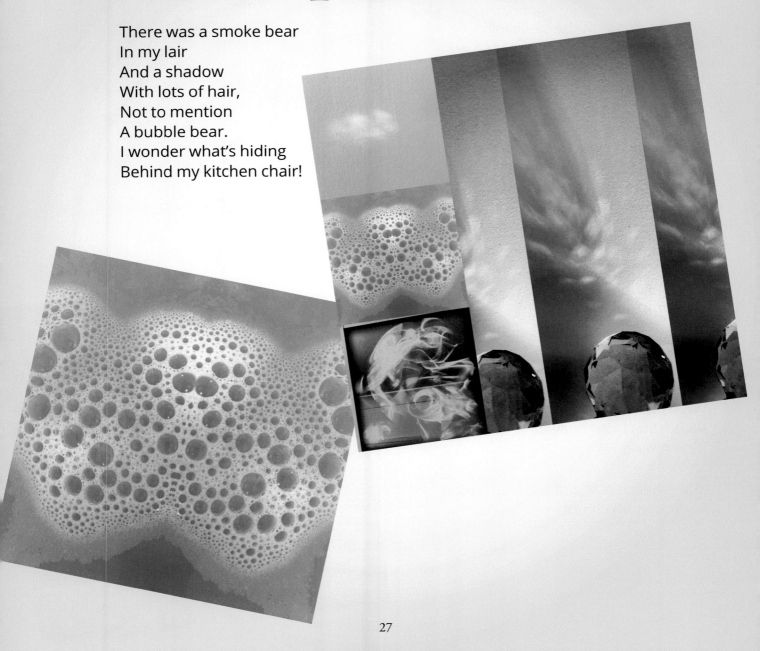

The garden.

Solar stars sit on the trellising,
Blossoms hide in the trees,
Solar hearts are in the laurel bush,
Roses a'climbing past me.

The pitchfork dug out the earth,
Loosening it from the half bake.
The basil has white flowers
The door mat needs a good shake.

My garden is full of hearts, flowers and stars,
No underground playground or black prison bars!
No basement coldness
Blocking the light,
No damp cold smell.
What a delight!

Instead the greenery enfolds
the secrets of the fairies.
Whilst the snails burrow and slime
Raindrops from heaven
Bide their time

In the heart, star and blossom shine
My soul doth climb!

I remember.

I remember the windy roads
Leading to the beach
With the stacked-up hay bales
Just out of reach.

I remember playing hide and seek
In the sand dunes
And the pillar boxes,
The feel of grass and
The whistling wind tunes.

I remember the cliffs slipping away,
Making sand castles and swimming,
In the rock pools,
And the broken clay of today.

I remember the sigh of the sea,
As another home fell
From crumbling sand. Glistening
Coppers sparkle in a wishing well.

I remember buying sweets with
My pocket money
And hiding from the Heffalumps and
Woozzles
Like, "Winnie the Pooh," and honey.

I remember the sparkle of the sun,
On water,
And the churn of boats through Blue
Green Algae-
A reluctant daughter.

I remember bonfire smell and glow,
Yellow and white daffodils,
Mud pies,
And the apple seeds lying low.

I remember ditches and dykes,
Farm grown vegetables,
Hard wooden chairs
And mercenary pikes.

The sunsets aglow
With pink and delight,
The sails full,
With evening light

Breath of dusk,
White musk
An elephant's tusk

I remember.

Faces in the Clouds.

Faces in the clouds:
White shrouds
Of animal face,
Displaced.

Faces in the clouds,
Like white lace,
Strewn across a white room,
Illuminated by the moon.

Faces in the clouds:
Faces I know
From stories at home
Seeds that are sown.

Faces in the clouds:
The white rabbit
Checking his watch
Or Alice skipping
With her merry gold locks.

Faces in the cracks.

Is it just me or can anyone see a little kitty?
Waiting to pounce on a tasty ounce of seagull
Waiting for a lull.

I can see them both
In the cracks of the wall

Looking at the Camden Town sign.
I'm just biding my time
Waiting for my train
Till the cat and bird
Disappear again.

Crab Apple.

Crab appley
Crab sapley
Crab apple happily
Overloaded with fruit,
Branches wild and free,

Delightful for you, for me
Rosy red and shiny yellow too.
A small treat for me, for you.
Plucking from the giving branch.

Like a nuzzling horse
Approaching a dusty ranch
In search of the gallop
And going through the hoop
Circling the loop.

And CRUNCH MUNCH

The horse bites
The crab apple
For his lunch.

It needed sugar,
He whinnies. He neighs.
But still a change from
Soot or hay.

Trotting off in haste
To enjoy the half-baked day,
To lay in hay,
Never to go astray.

The mountains observe this picture
like-

Blue Sky May.

Wolf.

Streamlined whiskers and pointy ears
Hide those forbidden tears
Dissipated over the
Treacherous years of
Deceit.
They say we sow what we reap.
I wonder what will appear at your wolfhound feet.
Distance howls and growls.
The fur keeps warmth at night
Despite the lack of light.

Watch out too! We bite!

Escape.

Escape into a book.
Take a look:
Can you see the vagabond in me?

Escape into a comic.
Ride on the villain's back.
See him as he strides.
It's humility he lacks.

Escape into a picture.
Feel the sharp of the wolf's fang.
Feel the princess hair.
To the dragon she sang.

Escape into the paint.
See heaven and hell,
Devil and Saint

Escape into the castle.
Sit by the fire,
The docile day unfolding
Like unwrapping a parcel.

Escape into the garden.
Trees a' galore
Snails, centipedes and robins
A blackbird I saw.

Escape into the picnic.
Sip the lemonade.
Watch the sunset
On parade.

Escape from imposed
Darkness, sadness and pain.

Escape from imposed
Embarrassment, criticism and shame.

Pink Rabbit.

Pink rabbit,
Not white rabbit
Like in Wonderland,
You're always on time.
Will you teach Mr White Rabbit your
habit?

So he can come and dine with me
Amongst the red and white roses
As the cherry tree poses
A glance like unspoken words
Lost in the breeze,
Whilst Daisy May
Plays on her knees
Searching hastily for woodlouse and
centipedes.

Pink rabbit,
How come you're not late?
Do you think that will affect your fate?

Being on time with the grind
Staring in front or looking behind.

"You're so PUNC-TU-AL!"
Sang Maggie McGal,

Singing your praise
All over the place.

Pink rabbit, your ears are so floppy
Five shades lighter than a glorious
poppy.

Your stare is a mirror
Straight into childhood
To play, to dance
If only you could,

But that time is gone for now
Until the next generation,
So hop on the train
And journey to the station.

Wave goodbye to the rabbit hole of
dark.
Look to the meadow and the great lark

With grace, this place,
I can see in your face.

Childhood once more.
Now open the door!

Lock of my life.

I turned the key in the lock of my life
And stood back in lace with grace
The lock of my life
Opened with a golden key
Just for me
It said, 'Drink me,'
But I'm not Alice!
Even though I have red and white roses
Inside and out.
Golden locks, a selfie and a pout.

I turned the lock of my life
And with delight I saw a sight

Free as a kite
With no bite
Like a twinkling solar light.

Twenty percent violent.

Slap a cake, slap a cake,
Builder's man. Build me a house
As fast as you can.
Pat it and slap it and stick with glee,
Then watch all the builders whilst
having tea

Slap a man, slap a man in his van
Slap him for making a stand

If he won't do it,
Who is his teacher?
Or did you forget
That little feature?

Slap a girl, slap a girl
Keeping you awake,
Intimidate, bully and
For whose sake?

Didn't anyone tell you when you slap
the world,
It slaps back?

Misery and fear land right in your lap.

Not to mention sadness, madness
destroying all gladness

As your slapping and clapping
Your life slips away.
The RAT that you are
Runs away from this Star.

Watch out for your ego; it can hardly fit
in the door.
Not forgetting that you're breaking the
law.

Smokey Bear.

I lit some incense,
And saw a paw,
Emerge above my living room door

It was a bear made out of smoke
He sat and watched me
But never spoke...

His nose was very sweet and round,
He didn't even make a sound,
It was lucky I turned around...

Because with the smoke he was gone,
Before I could even take a yawn,
I waved goodbye and took his pic,

And there he was
Click at te click!
He reminded me of a toy called Big Ted

Full of cuddles,
On my wardrobe he shed,
Big Ted hair and Big Ted fur,
Sometimes I thought I heard him purr,
A bear sort of purr like brrr and grrr.

Well thank you smokey bear for
popping round,
Great to make your acquaintance,
Without a sound...

I hope to see you again some day!
I would really love for you to play,
With Big Ted, but I'll have to find him

He could be in the attic or under the
stair
Or in the bedroom, Or at the fair!

I played with him so long ago
It was in my childhood and so
I will ask him he wants to come for tea

And light some incense
Once more
And really hope to see your paw
Emerge above my sitting room door!

My plea to writing.

By boat and by sea,
All will hear my plea,
To be seen and be heard,
Like a nightingale bird,
flying high above rain,
No vain, pain or shame.

Writing is my dream,
Pen and paper is my team,
So over mountain and green
Boat, air and steam..

My words will be read
Yes that's what I said !

Pictures to behold,
Copies will be sold,
Into the hearts and mind
Of every human kind.

To pledge to be free,
Controllers will see,
And leave in haste,
After having a taste,

Every picture speaks,
Just like every boat leaks,

Writing in the sky
Flying so high
Over wind, over dale,
Over mist, through the hale,
For the sale

Lots of words
For lots of hearts
Lots of pictures
for lots of sharks

Bobbing along the energy field
Magnetic energy will I yield

They didn't believe me
Well let them look now

Seeds in words I have sown,
And now to the plough,
Through weed and through seed,
Helping to feed

The right pasture
The world you can master,
Through sculpting and plaster,
Avoiding shipwreck disaster

The white clouds can see,
And the buzzing yellow bee,
All evil will flee
All sticky and tarry
Away from Gold Starry!

Merriment we will make,
In the blue day's half bake,
The ripe Sun's glories

Shines through all my stories..

Mexican eating cat.

Mexican eating cat
Licked the plate clean
Spicy foods
Keeping him lean.

Mexican eating cat
Ate up the curry
And all of the syrup
In a flurry of hurry.

Mexican eating cat
Sat on the mat
Licking his lips
Looking for ships

To sail the seven seas
People to please
Waiting for rats
And waiting for cheese

To appease all the dogs
And even the hogs
And write all the blogs
In mist or in fogs

Mexican eating cat had a royal name
Georgie and second name Miley

Valued very highly
Not devious or
Acting very slyly

He travelled the world.
With gypsies scarfs pearled.
Not hunched or not curled.

But dancing and twirled.

Through the clouds
Through the crowds
Past all the shrouds

Of other people's dreams
Coming apart at the seams
Running along ships beams

Like wispy angel wings
As the nightingale sings..

Lies lies and lies

Lies and lies and lies-
Like poo on flies,
Why do you tell lies?
Manipulate, lies,
I'm breaking the ties
with you, phew.

Lies and lies and lie,
Did your integrity die?
With a half baked line
Uttered when dined-
Half signed-
Resigned with the better part
Of your heart gone then tried to make a
start with -

Lies lies lies,
Broken soul ties like horse flys buzz
Over yesterday's fuzz
Getting rid of you
is a must -

What do you get out of telling lies lies
lies?
As your dandruff falls into your grub
And you eat it like a sweet-

Grotesque and foul
Nobody's pal
but your own-

Lies lies lies,
Knot you in ties,
Energy absorbing the cloud dense skies
Who will buy your lie?

Before you die alone like a stone-
No one on the phone-

To hear your lies, lies, lies.

God loves a tryer

God loves a tryer
And will reward them
As they climb higher and higher,
A high flyer.

God loves a tryer
And will smile on you,
In different ways
The sun's ripe gaze.

God loves a tryer.
Pictures and writing
He will admire
Romance, horror and satire.

God loves a tryer
Like the wind and the fire

A footprint stampede
Galloping old shire.

God loves a tryer
And forgives the liar
Weaving webs of deceit
At his glorious feet.

God loves a tryer
Through wind and through rain,
Through darkness and light,
Happiness and pain.

As life gallops on
Through the passage of time.
Envy defeated,
Loving hearts shine.

Printed in the United States
By Bookmasters